CONTENTS

HEALMOTIONS

Unwrapping the Mummy Layers

Dr. Demetria Springfield Banks

Unless otherwise indicated, all Scripture quotations are taken from the King James Version of the Bible. *The Holy Bible. Old and New Testaments in the King James Version.* Copyright© 1970 by Thomas Nelson, Inc.

Copyright 2014. Demetria S. Banks. All rights reserved. No part of this work may be reproduced or copied in any form or by any means – graphic, electronic or mechanical; including photocopying, recording, taping or use of any information retrieval system without the express written consent of the author.

INTRODUCTION

All of us have experienced some type of emotional pain during our journey in life, whether it was from a harsh word spoken to us or a cruel act done to us. Indeed, emotional pain is a universal issue affecting people everywhere – regardless to who they are, their status, their occupations, race or nationality. There are even individuals involved in ministry who suffer with emotional wounds – trying to help others, while they, themselves, are in need of emotional healing.

Some emotional wounds heal with the passage of time. For example, we typically can bounce back from a "not so nasty" word of anger spoken to us or a "not so nasty" offense done to us by an upset spouse, relative, friend, classmate or co-worker. On the other hand, there are situations that can cause deep emotional scarring. A person does not heal easily with these type wounds. They are not able to bounce back and as a result experience years of emotional turmoil and pain to the point where it impairs their ability to live a normal life.

Some attempt suicide, while others turn to drug abuse, alcohol abuse or anything they feel will help numb the pain of the emotional anxiety they are experiencing.

In talking with many individuals who suffer with deep emotional wounds, I find that many desire to be free. There's a small inner voice on the inside of them crying out "Help me! Help me!" These individuals want to come out from behind their prison walls. They are tired of not enjoying life to the fullest. They, especially Christians, know that there is a better way for them, but for various reasons are unable to grasp this better way. They are like "mummies," walking around wrapped in layer on top of layer of emotional bondage.

The word of God lets us know that it is NOT God's desire that we be held captive by our emotions in any kind of way. It is not His desire that we live a dry, joyless life. It is not His desire that we live in fear – afraid to reach out to others; afraid to enjoy life because of current or past experiences. Indeed, the word of God lets us know that Jesus came that we might have an abundant life.

The thief cometh not, but for to steal, and to kill, and to destroy: I am come that they might have life, and that they might have it more abundantly. John 10:10

God certainly wants all of us to be every wit whole – spiritually, mentally, physically, and emotionally.

There was a man in the bible who was described as impotent and in this condition for 38 years. Can you imagine that! He suffered paralysis for 38 long years. Jesus asked him one day in John 5:6, "Wilt thou be made whole?" I can picture this man being full of mixed emotions at this point. On one hand, I'm sure he was overjoyed to hear that he has the opportunity to be made whole after suffering for such a long time. But on the other hand, astonished, pinching himself asking if this was a dream since he had missed the opportunity to be healed on so many occasions.

Nevertheless, Jesus commanded him to rise and take up his bed and walk. The Bible says IMMEDIATELY, in verse 9, the man was made whole! Now, imagine Jesus asking you this very same question on today, "Wilt thou be made whole?" Although this man was in need of a physical healing, it is also God's will that we be emotionally whole as well.

Many people who suffer with emotional injury also seem unable to grasp God's truths that inner healing belongs to them and that God's love for them is unconditional. Satan has blinded their minds to these truths.

In whom the god of this world hath blinded the minds of them which believe not, lest the light of the glorious gospel of Christ, who is the image of God, should shine unto them. 2 Corinthians 4:4

Although this scripture specifically refers to satan blinding the mind of men and women from receiving the good news of Jesus Christ, it can be applied to satan's hindering work in general.

I pray that this book, *Healmotions: Unwrapping the Mummy Layers*, penetrate your deepest thoughts and longings, helping you to grasp the reality of God's will of COMPLETE deliverance for you. I pray that it usher you into the freedom that you have desired for so long. I also pray that God uses it to open your mind and understanding that you may comprehend the breadth, length, depth and height of God's love for you (Ephesians 3:18).

Chapter One

The Mummy Layers

The Sources

The sources of emotional wounds are wide and varied. I will list some here. However, as you read through this list, others may come to your mind.

A person can suffer emotional wounds from a bad marriage, a divorce, or an affair. Situations such as these can be so hurtful for some until they struggle immensely with depression, regret, loneliness, low self-esteem and heartache. Many times some lack the strength and the will to bounce back.

Emotional wounds can also be caused by violent acts such as rape, abduction, or physical violence. Without a doubt, a violet act such as rape can cause a considerable amount of emotional scarring for the victim. Consider the story of Tamar's rape in 2 Samuel 13.

The story begins by telling us that Tamar was a *fair* (meaning she was beautiful), young girl. Her brother, Amnon, desired her so until it made him sick because he couldn't have her. One day Amnon devised a scheme by pretending that he was ill only to have his sister cook and bring him some food. When Tamar brought him the food, he asked her to lay with him. Tamar refused so Amnon raped her (verse 14). After the rape, the bible goes on to say, that Amnon hated his sister with a greater passion than the love he originally felt for her. Rather than do right by his sister and marry her, as according to the law in Deuteronomy 22:28, he sent his sister away in disgrace. Imagine the emotional turmoil and pain that this caused for Tamar! She was disgraced, abandoned, humiliated, and destroyed by an event beyond her control. With out a doubt, emotional devastation such as this can cause pain for an individual that can last for the rest of their life, if it is tucked away and not properly dealt with.

Not only are violent acts such as this a source of emotional pain for the victim, but they are also a source of emotional pain for the individual who witnesses them. For example, a child who sees his or her mother physically abused repeatedly by the father, can suffer emotional damage from witnessing this act. If it is a girl child, she may grow up hating all men, thinking that they are all alike, inhibiting her ability to form lasting relationships. Some, once becoming an adult, end up falling in love with men who treat them in the same manner as their father treated their mother. If it's a boy child, he may grow up thinking this is how all women should be treated by men, thereby affecting his ability to develop positive, lasting relationships as well.

Consider also the emotional trauma that can be caused for the individual who witnesses someone murdered by another, particularly if it is someone close to them. Unable to get the event out of their mind, the individual deals with posttraumatic stress, fear, has difficulty sleeping, eating, thinking, and concentrating.

Emotional wounds can also result from verbal abuse, from someone repeatedly calling another person derogatory or degrading names. Or from an individual repeatedly hailing insults at another. I call this "down talking" a person. We have also experienced the inside hurt to some degree of being called an ugly name by someone. But for individuals who are subject to this type of abuse for a long period of time, the effects can be devastating.

One example of down talking is a parent telling a child that they will never be anything or amount to anything so much so until the child becomes a failure even in his or her own eyesight. Another example, is an individual who's in a relationship with another, whether that relationship is a friendship, courtship, marriage, or family relationship who is repeatedly called degrading terms such as "useless," "good for nothing," "stupid," or "dumb." The pain of years of this type of abuse can be traumatic for some, spilling over into their adulthood, negatively affecting his or her self-esteem, confidence, and ability to form meaningful relationship with others.

I would like to point out here that although the wounds from mental abuse are not as apparent to the eye as those from physical abuse, their effects can be just as traumatic. They too can cause an individual to struggle with depression, extreme mood swings, become withdrawn, low self-esteem, low confidence, etc.

Emotional damage can also be caused by a person spreading "vicious" rumors about another. Many of us have experienced and witnessed the emotional turmoil caused by gossip. Not only is such an act damaging to a person's emotions, but it can also ruin marriages and other significant relationships.

Bullying can be another source of emotional damage for some individuals. Even cyber-bullying can have a negative impact on an individual's emotions. Most of the time when we think of bullying, we think of school bullies pestering our children, our grandchildren, or other family members. However, bullying can also take place in the home, on the job, and in social organizations. The affect of bullying can be so extreme until it can cause a person to commit suicide. They feel that there is no way out and no one to turn to. Even sometimes telling others that they are being bullied doesn't stop this damaging behavior from occurring again and again to them.

Still, another person can suffer emotional pain by the rejection or ostracism (any act of banishing, shunning, ignoring or excluding) that he or she has received from others – family members, co-workers, friends, classmates, or other significant persons. Even "small" situations involving rejection can cause significant emotional pain. Guy Weinch, in his article, *Rejection is More Powerful than You Think*, states that "Many of the rejections that we experience are comparatively mild and our injuries heal over time. But when left untreated, even the wounds created by mild rejections can become "infected" and cause psychological complications that seriously impact our mental well-being."

Weinch also discusses in this article the results of a "ball tossing experiment," in which three participants are involved. Two of the participants are research confederates, while the third participant is the subject. The experiment involves all three participants sitting in a waiting room. The first confederate picks up a ball and throws it to the second confederate. The second confederate then throws it to the subject in the study. This goes on for about two rounds.

On the third round, instead of the second confederate throwing the ball to the subject, he throws it back to confederate number one, purposely excluding the subject out. Now most of us would say, "Please. Who cares about a stupid ball not being thrown to me?" However, psychologists found that people (the subjects) consistently reported feeling **significant** emotional pain as a result of being excluded from the ball-tossing game. Weinch also goes on

13

to say that "If such a trivial experience can elicit sharp emotional pain (as well as drops in mood and even self-esteem), we can begin to appreciate how painful truly meaningful rejections often are." Without a doubt, rejection or ostracism can be devastating emotionally to an individual.

At the core of rejection or ostracism is the thought by the individual that he or she is not good enough or is a bad person, which explains to them why they are being rejected. Consider the child who is constantly rejected by his or her mother or father. He or she will grow up living in a shell, afraid to trust others and afraid to form close relationships with others for fear of rejection. Rejection or ostracism can cause such a hurtful pain that it can spin a person into years of hurt and suffering with low self-esteem, or low self-worth, and insecurity. The distress of rejection can also cause an individual to feel detached, lonely, as well as harbor feelings of anger, resentment, and unforgiveness – all of which can negatively impact the physical health of the individual.

The negative effects of rejection can be powerful!

Some of us have come across the paths of those who have or are experiencing emotional distress resulting from losing a love one or close friend through death. Naturally, when our love ones die we hurt. We feel sorrowful and our hearts are broken. But when this pain inhibits our ability to function normally in life – several days of not eating; continued poor performance at work or school; refusing to leave the house because life doesn't seem worth living anymore, then it becomes an emotional problem that needs to be dealt with.

Others have experienced emotional trauma due to loss of their material possessions or even the loss of their jobs. Unable to cope, some end up living on the streets. Once productive, clean-cut members of society, now homeless, living on the streets unable to bounce back from the losses they have suffered. Recall the Stock Market Crash of 1929. The emotional trauma due to financial loss was so great that there were reported cases of suicide.

Have you experienced a loss so great that you contemplated suicide? If so, know that God commands you to live! Ezekiel 16:6

The biblical character, Job, suffered emotional wounding due to the loss of his material possessions and family. Many of us are familiar with his story in the book of Job. The Lord allowed the devil to take everything Job had – his home, his children, his property, his livestock, even Job's wife walked out on him. Job was cut to the core so badly that he cursed the day he was born (Job 3:1) and wished he was dead (Job 3:11). This is exactly how many feel that have been deeply emotionally wounded. Their inner pain eats away at them and cuts them to the core. They experience a deep sorrow

15

that they cannot shake. They even wish they were dead and as I mentioned earlier, some commit suicide. Fortunately for Job, this is not how his story ended. With God in the equation, he was able to bounce back!

I have even spoken with individuals whose source of emotional distress resulted from being a victim in a natural disaster. So profound and devastating was the event that they witnessed – the lost of many lives and total destruction of businesses, churches, and everything they and others had ever worked for, that it pushed them into a world of fear, shock, anxiety, and insecurity. Just to talk about the event is enough to rekindle feelings of fear and anxiety in these individuals that they can't seem to shake. Indeed, they may have survived the event, but not the emotional turmoil it has caused.

Even an individual's failures – whether from a failed relationship, career, business venture, or scholastic achievement, can become a source of emotional turmoil for them. Taunted and overwhelmed with frustrations, regret, unforgiveness, and disappointments brought on by the failure, this person becomes emotionally wounded, unable to move forward.

Let me not fail to mention that church hurt is another source of emotional wounds for some. What makes church hurt even more piercing for many, is because the church is suppose to be a safe haven for people who have been hurt and the people in the church are suppose to be instruments of healing, as oppose to instruments of hurt and pain. Whether the hurt was from rejection, exclusion, mistreatment, being lied on, ridiculed or manipulation, depending on the nature or the degree of hurt, a person may or may not bounce back emotionally from a church hurt. Some not able to successfully cope with a church hurt, have left the church. Others have not left the church, but have become very critical and cynical toward the church. Still others have been wounded so badly that they have turned away from God.

As difficult as it may be, we must all know that no church hurt is worth us losing our soul salvation! When we encounter church hurt, we must remind ourselves that God is not the author of the hurt, pain or confusion. Turning our backs on Him is not the answer. Taking matters into our own hands is not the answer either. More often than not, when we take matters into our own hands and attempt to "settle the score," we do ourselves more harm than good. Usually our methods of settling the score are contrary to God's word. Anything contrary to God's word is sure to spell more disappointment, more hurt, more anger, and more emotional bruising.

I agree that it is very sad that the enemy is able to use some of those in the church to be instruments of hurt. However our late pastor, Bishop G.E. Patterson, would tell us that no matter how bad things appear to be in the church, it is still safer to be in the house of the Lord rather than outside the house of the Lord. As the bible says, it is better for you not to have known the way of salvation than to have come into the knowledge then turn your back on God (2 Peter 2:21).

Have you ever experienced emotional wounding because of a church hurt?

Oh the list goes on and on relative to the many events, circumstances or situations that can cause emotional trauma for individuals. This pain for some can be so intense and lasting that it interferes with their ability to think rationally, to make sound decisions, to sleep, to eat and function normally in life. Unable to get a grip on things or on their feelings, some develop health problems such as high blood pressure and ulcers. Dr. Joseph Mercola in his article, *5 Tips for Recovering from Emotional Pain,* wrote:

> Emotional pain often exacts a greater toll on your quality of life than physical pain. The stress and negative emotions associated with any trying event can even lead to physical pain and disease." In fact, emotional stress is linked to health problems including chronic inflammation, lowered immune function, increased blood pressure, altered brain chemistry, increased tumor growth and more. Of course, emotional pain can be so severe that it interferes with your ability to enjoy

18

life and, in extreme cases, may even make you question whether your life is worth living." (*www.articles.mercola.com*)

Chapter Two
The Mummy Layers

The mummy layers represent the "residue" left from each ugly, hurtful and damaging experience that you have experienced in life. It represents each unhealed wound in your life; each morsel of unforgiveness, hatred, bitterness, fear, or embarrassment that has prevented you from living and enjoying life to the fullest.

Let's discuss some of the common layers emotionally scarred individuals deal with. Some individuals who have been emotionally wounded are wrapped in the layer of **shock**. It happened unexpectedly and they felt powerless against it. They can't believe such a cruel act happened to them, particularly in the case of rape or molestation. Although the event may have happened several years ago, they still are in shock, continuously searching for reasons as to why it happened, was it something that they did or said, or even why God allowed it to happen.

Others struggle emotionally with the shock of losing someone close to them, particularly if this person died prematurely, suddenly or violently. They find themselves months, even years later still trying to come to grips with the person's death. A person experiencing this type of shock can have trouble eating, sleeping at night, concentrating and other detrimental feelings.

Still others who are emotionally wounded may be wrapped in the layers of **guilt and blame**. Somehow they blame themselves for what happened to them. If only they would have done or said something differently, they reason, then this terrible act wouldn't have happened to them. They also feel guilty because they allowed the abuse or mistreatment to continue for a long period of time without reaching out for help or removing themselves from the situation. They feel so guilty that they are unable to enjoy life, their relationship with others and their relationship with God. Guilt becomes a weight on them, weighing them down day in and day out, depriving them of peace and joy.

I must point out here that not all guilt is bad. If we feel guilty for offending our brother or sister, then guilt is not a bad thing. We should feel remorseful or sorrowful if we have hurt someone in any kind of way. God gave us a conscious. He said in 1 John 3:21, *"For if our heart condemn us, God is greater than our heart, and knoweth all things."* Yet if guilt becomes our constant companion, where we wake up with it every morning, and go to bed with it every night, can't think clearly or move on with life, then guilt becomes a layer of bondage rather than a moral guide for our actions.

Still others feel guilty because of a bad decision they made. This can be in the case of a woman who decides to remain in a physically or emotionally abusive relationship with a man, although her life is on a down spiral because of it.

Those who have been emotionally damaged are also wrapped in the layer of **shame** - ashamed of what happened to them; ashamed that they are unable to get past it; ashamed that they don't have enough faith to receive God's deliverance; and ashamed that if someone finds out about it they will look at them in another way.

Others suffering from emotional pain, are wrapped in a layer of *low self-esteem, low self-worth or low self-confidence*. The abuse, the rejection, the ongoing degrading and derogatory remarks and other malicious things they have experienced in life have caused them to feel poorly about themselves. They see themselves as "ugly," even if they are physically attractive. They are quick to reject any compliment you give them. No matter how you try to point out the good character traits about them or things that they are good at doing, they refuse to accept it. As soon as something good is said about them, they quickly shake their head in disagreement saying, "No, no I'm not."

The emotional pain for those suffering with low self-esteem can be so great that they believe that not even God can love them or use them for His service.

Because of their low opinion of themselves, their expectations are low. They

22

don't believe in themselves. They don't expect good things to come from them or happen to them. They smile when they hear good news about others, while thinking to themselves that "This won't ever happen to me." Don't be shocked if they are surprised when they produce, for example, a great report at work or make a decision that turns out to be beneficial to themselves or to others. Their poor self-esteem constantly tells them that nothing good can come from them.

In addition, because of their low self-esteem, they don't expect much out of life. Low self-esteem also causes them to have trouble speaking up for themselves or sharing their opinions when talking with others. "Who will listen to what I have to say," they think to themselves. "I'm a nobody."

Furthermore, some are overly concerned about with what others think about them. They are "people pleasers" in every sense of the word. They go overboard in trying to please others and trying not to "step on other's toes." If someone takes offense to something they do or say, they are quick to "overly" apologize, apologizing over and over again.

I have found that some of the individuals who are wrapped with the layer of low self-esteem feel so **unlovable**. Their daily thoughts center around, "No one could love me. I'm just a nothing." "I'm an emotional wreck." "I don't deserve God's love. I don't deserve anyone's love." "Who could ever love me, especially once they find out what happened to me?" It is certainly difficult to get them to see that they are worth loving and worthy of receiving other's love, care and concern. They really want to love, they want to accept the love others desire to give, but cannot.

Low self-esteem also causes them to be easy manipulated and controlled by others. These individuals further contribute to the person's already low self-esteem by being verbally abusive to them, insulting them, rejecting them when they don't do something that they want them to do in an attempt to keep them "under their thumbs." They work overtime instilling in an already emotional wounded person untruths such as they are nothing without them; they cannot make it without them; that they need them in order to survive.

Another layer of bondage wrapped around those who have been emotionally bruised is **denial**. We call it "sweeping things under the rug." What happened to them was so painful, so distressful, that in order to cope with it, they deny it happened. Denial is a coping mechanism to help them get through each day. To admit that it happened, only brings back pain and feelings that they want to forget. Yet, denying the problem causes more problems.

Denial prevents the healing virtue of God from flowing in the individual's life.

How can God heal an individual if he or she denies there is a problem, a scar, or a wound? We will talk more about this later.

Fear, is another layer wrapped around some of those who are emotionally wounded. They are fearful of forming relationships with others because a person they trusted violated their trust. Psychologists refer to this as *emotional detachment.* Emotional detachment is defined by *Wikipedia* as: 1) The inability to connect with others emotionally, as well as a means of dealing with anxiety by preventing certain situations that trigger it, and 2) The decision by an individual to avoid engaging emotional connections, rather than an inability or difficult in doing so, typically for personal, social or other reasons. So emotional detachment for an emotionally scarred person can come from both the individual's inability to connect with others as well as the individual's decision to avoid connecting with others in order protect himself or herself from being hurt again.

Emotionally wounded individuals also are fearful of others finding out what happened to them. If others find out, they reason, then they will withdraw from them. Fear can also lead to irrational thinking – for example, thinking someone is out to get them, stalking them, or constantly watching them.

Now, we all know that fear in many cases is a natural response to a bad event or events. For example, if someone breaks into our home, then naturally for a while we may become fearful or apprehensive when returning home from work or church, etc. However, if fear grips or paralyzes us to the point where we become paranoid or cannot function normally at work, home or at school or any other social gathering, then fear becomes a layer of bondage holding us captive and needs to be dealt with.

Pretense is also a layer wrapped around those who are in emotional pain. They pretend that they are happy, yet on the inside they are falling apart. On the outside they are well-dressed and appear they have it together, but on the inside, they are an emotional wreck! On the inside, they are bombarded with guilt, bitterness, shame, low self-esteem, regret and the list goes on. They walk around with a mask on, not wanting others to know their story, not wanting others to know that they have been badly hurt by another, particularly if it was hurt inflicted by someone that was suppose to love or protect them. They are the "silent sufferers." As Joyce Meyer wrote in her book *Beauty for Ashes*, "I was so miserable and unhappy. Yet, like so many people, I pretended that everything was fine."

Others may be wrapped in a layer of **depression**; some to the point where they are in need of professional help. Depression here is more than a gloomy, empty feeling that last for about a week. It lingers for several weeks, months, for some, years. It is a dark, heavy gloominess and hopelessness that the individual cannot shake or snap out of. They dread getting out of bed in the morning. They want to stay locked in at home, desiring to be around no one. A word of encouragement from the pastor, the evangelist, or others may provide "temporary" uplifting only to have this person fall back into the heaviness they were feeling. They believe that there is no light at the end of the tunnel. There is no way out. They feel locked in. They don't want to feel that way, but they lack the energy to push themselves to snap out of it.

Many emotional wounded people walk around tied to the layer of **unforgiveness** – unable to forgive their perpetuators; unable to forgive themselves; angry and unable to forgive even God. They know that forgiveness is the right thing to do, yet they struggle to forgive. A struggle that we can understand, considering what happened. Think for a moment about the woman who was raped; the child who was molested; the wife who was battered to the point where she spent weeks in the hospital; the husband whose wife left him for his close friend. Indeed, unforgiveness can be challenging to any of us, and in particular with those who are emotionally bruised. Yet, not being able to forgive locks the door of emotional healing for an individual.

Most certainly being able to forgive is key to receive inner healing.

Forgiving those who have trespassed against us (Matthew 6:12) keeps us from walking in anger, hatred, malice and bitterness, releasing us to receiving the healing God has for us. It releases us to move on in life without carrying around the extra baggage. It releases God's hand to operate on our behalf to heal and mend us. It also protects our physical health as we release the anger, rage and bitterness we feel inside. Forgiveness is such an important key in receiving inner healing, that I will talk more on it later in this book. It is a necessity. It is a must.

As ironic as it sounds, some won't even forgive themselves for what happened to them. They walk around in **condemnation** (another mummy layer), beating themselves up over and over about the situation. They fail to realize and take advantage of the forgiveness that Jesus provides to them and to those who has trespassed against them. It's difficult for them to accept such truths as 1 John 1:9 and Romans 8:1. 1 John 1:9 says, *If we confess our sins, he is faithful and just to forgive us our sins, and to cleanse us from all unrighteousness.* Romans 8:1 says, *"There is therefore now no condemnation to them which are in Christ Jesus, who walk not after the flesh, but after the Spirit.*

A **feeling of hopelessness** is yet another common layer wrapping those who have been damaged emotionally. Since it is difficult for them to see why God or anyone would love or care for them, its difficult to see that He or anyone else wants to help them. Even if God wants to help, they think that what they are going through is so beyond repair, that He

28

cannot. Yes, some have read scriptures that state nothing is too hard for God; that God can do the impossible. Yet, they don't believe those scriptures are for them. As a result, they accept their condition as being a way of life for themselves.

What I have just discussed are just a few of many layers that wrap those who are emotionally wounded. Even as I presented these, others may have come to your mind. The thing to remember is that regardless to what the layer is, it can wreck havoc in so many ways in the lives of those living with it. So profound is the damage of an emotional wound until it can put some into a tail spin where they never fully recover. For others, it can cause them to turn to ungodly addictions such as – alcohol addiction, drug addiction, sex or pornography addiction, spending addiction and even eating binges, to name a few. Psychologists term this type of coping as *escapism*. Even knowing that such addictions will only cause more pain and suffering for them isn't enough to stop them from using them to escape the pain that they feel. Some even turn to self-mutilation, cutting themselves as a way to escape their inner pain. Others can be driven to the point of deadly rage.

Without a doubt, people who have been emotionally wounded are even capable of committing crimes.

Prompted by built-up rage, they seek revenge on those who have caused them harm.

29

For example, the boyfriend who is unable to get past his broken heart because his girlfriend breaks up with him and moves on with her life. Unable to cope with the rage, anger, hurt and bitterness built up inside of him, he becomes beside himself, stalks her, then murders her, even then not realizing the seriousness of his actions because his rage has gotten the best of him.

Or think about the co-worker, who "snaps" because he felt he was wrongly terminated from his job of many years. He returns to the job, armed and dangerous, shooting everyone he feels is responsible – even including those who were not responsible. Certainly, the consequence of emotional hurts or emotional scars can be devastating. So powerful that some have suffered from nervous breakdowns.

Chapter Three

Living with those who are Emotionally Wounded

A person who lives with an individual who has suffered emotional trauma can find themselves many times at wits end – ready to pull their hair out! This can be a very trying situation for them as well. No doubt, they have tried unsuccessfully to talk to this person over and over again, to reason with this person, to seek out avenues of help for this person, but to no avail.

They have also tried to convince the individual that God doesn't intend for their situation to be a way for life them. That they don't have to be a victim to their past. That God has a better way for them. But, regardless to how hard they try or how convincing they may sound, they are unable to penetrate the mummy layers wrapping the individual. At times, they are somewhat successful in inspiring a little hope and faith through the use of God's word. But, more often than not this is a "temporary fix" because the individual lacks the faith, persistence and strength needed to permanently overcome their situation.

If the person suffering is a Christian, this makes the situation even more frustrating to those living with them. It is difficult for them to understand how the person can be both Christian and walking in emotional bondage at the same time, month after month, year after year. The person living with the emotionally bound Christian frantically ask himself or herself questions such as, "Why can't they get over this they are suppose to be Christian?" What's their problem?" They also say statements such as "They go to church." "They know the God's word." "They know that God is able to completely deliver them and that He doesn't want to see them in distress!" So in exasperation and frustration, they cry out "Lord, help!"

To you I say, yes many Christians suffering with emotional wounds know God's word. They know what He can do. They know that He is a strong deliverer. Yet the pain, the scars, the hurt, the anger, the disappointment, the guilt, the regrets, the unforgiveness, and other frustrations that they deal with on a daily basis smother out any faith that they can grab a hold to.

As angry as you may be or as frustrated and helpless as you may feel, you must come to grips with the fact that the enemy has a strong hold over your love one, Christian or non-Christian, which means it is not something easy they can get out of. Deliverance is not impossible, but not easily obtained. The condition they are in overpowers any type of sound reasoning, hope or inspiration that comes their way. Although the way you feel is valid, the strong hold(s) in your love ones' life prevents him or her from accepting and holding on to God's truths.

I remember asking myself similar questions and making similar statements when dealing with various love ones in my family who were emotionally wounded. "Why can't they beat this?" I would ask myself and God. "Why can't they overcome this? They attend church all the time." "What is holding them back?" "What's in the way?" Sometimes I would say to God, "Now, come on God. I know You are able and are a prayer answering God. Yet it doesn't seem as if You are answering my prayers on my love one's behalf. I'm tired of dealing with this. I'm tired of seeing them suffer. Surely there is a way of escape for them!"

I'm going to share a few things that God dealt with me on in dealing with those who are emotionally bruised in one's family. God told me that a lot of times in prayer, we pray for relief of the manifestations of the problem that we see in the natural – the depression, the guilt; the sadness, the fear, the mental instability, etc. However, He told me that we must pray that He deals with the problem at the root, not the outward symptoms of the problem. Although symptoms of an issue manifest in different ways, there is always an underlying root cause that's the source of all of the symptoms. If we desire to see real deliverance for our love ones or others who suffer emotionally, then we must pray that God get to the root of the problem and cut the problem off at the root. Then the person whom we are praying for can receive complete deliverance and healing.

Dealing with the root of an issue is crucial to uprooting emotional damage permanently.

God also told me that when dealing with those who are emotionally wounded in our families, we must have PATIENCE, in every sense of the word. I am not talking about a week or two of patience. But we must have real patience, as we ask God to work His work on behalf of our love ones. Of course, this is easier said than done! But if we are going to be of help to our love ones who are suffering, we must do it!

Healing from emotional trauma takes time and patience. It will not be overnight. Now sometimes God delivers instantaneously, but many times He delivers in the process of time. You must expect days of ups and downs; days of slow progress and in some cases, no progress; days of taking a step forward, then days of taking two steps backwards. Frustrations, hurt, retaliation and anger will come to you, but in order to better help your love one, it is necessary that you push through all of these and remain patient in their healing process. Remember, longsuffering is a fruit of the Spirit (Galatians 6:1).

You must also be patient with their pace. Remember everyone responds to trauma differently. What takes one a short time to understand and begin to implement, may take another more time to understand and implement. Resist the urge to compare their pace with someone else's pace. It will only set them back. Although two situations may "appear" to be the same, no two situations are exactly alike.

Remember when I mentioned earlier that I asked myself questions like, "Why can't they beat this, etc.?" Well, when dealing with the emotionally bruised, to you things seem rational, that if the person does this, and believes that and if they confess this, and confess that, then deliverance will come. But what we must note here is that damaged emotions can and does thrust an individual out of rational thinking, where they can't see past their hurt, their pain, their wound. They have sunken so low in the valley of their wound until they are knocked out of the reality of their thinking and their situation.

Part of being patient, is asking God to give you a better and clearer understanding of what the person is going through. Ask God to help you view their situation from their lenses in order to give you a better understanding of what they are thinking, of what they are experiencing. Indeed, you will have to continuingly ask God to give you patience, patience and more patience because it will take patience to help both of you through this trying situation. It will take patience to help you maintain your sanity, sort of speak. You don't want to fluster yourself more by acting impatiently to a person who seems to "not get it." Neither do you want to cause them more grief and sorrow by being impatient toward them during the healing process.

Also, resolve within yourself to be there for them - to talk, to listen, not judge them. Resist the urge to try to pressure them into talking about what's going on with them or why they are behaving a certain way. Although you may be well meaning in your intent, if your family member is not ready to talk, he or she can find become easily offended by your actions. Some find it difficult and embarrassing to talk about what happened. Some are simply not ready to share their experience. So don't try to force them to open up to you, but let them know that you are there whenever they are ready. In their own time, they will share what they want you to know.

In order to better help you live with someone emotionally bruised in your family, you can also educate yourself by doing research online, at the library or wherever God may lead you in order to give you a clearer understanding of what's going on. There are numerous articles written on those dealing with emotional damage – how it affects them; how it affects those close to them; how it causes them to feel and so forth. As I stated in the introduction, emotional damage is a problem that affects people everywhere, from all walks of life. Doing research will also provide you with additional resources to help this individual.

At times your love one may become very agitated, lash out and say mean things to you. They may even become withdrawn. Don't take it personally. I think it's our natural inclination that when someone takes offense to us, especially when we are trying to help, that we take it personally. However, taking it personally can cause you to say or do something you may later regret. Remember their feelings and actions are a result of the emotional pain they feel, and may not have anything to do with you. So again, try your best to see beyond their behavior and keep in mind that there is a hurting individual inside.

You can also try to encourage them to get out and live a little. Don't push. Just try. Offer to take them out to see a play, the movies, play tennis or go to dinner, etc. This will help take their attention and focus off of their emotional pain. They may or may not take you up on your offer. But it's worth a try.

Above all, pray, pray and pray again. Pray God gives you the right word, at the right time that will help your love one. Sometimes we have the right word, but it might not be the right time. Proverbs 15:23 says, *A man hath joy by the answer of his mouth: and a word spoken in due season, how good is it!"* Pray that God will help you to remain patient. Pray that the enemy is rebuked and your love's ones understanding and heart is opened and receptive to receive God's love, God's forgiveness, and God's healing power.

Some situations will require fasting and prayer (Matthew 17:21). Even if you have already fasted and prayed and nothing has changed, remain steadfast and unmoveable in this good work. Your labor is not in vain (1 Corinthians 15:58). Remember Jesus Christ is the same yesterday, today and forevermore (Hebrews 13:8). That same powered that healed the feeble minded, the broken hearted, and the bruised back in biblical days is the same power that is available to heal your love one today!

Chapter 4

Lord, I Need Healing

Emotional wounds that have not been healed can cause physical, mental, emotional and spiritual problems. They can also negatively impact an individual's marriage, job and school performance. In addition, they can drive an individual to do something that they would not otherwise do.

As I mentioned in the introduction, many individuals suffering from emotional damage desire to be free, but are not for one reason or another. They appear to be functioning normally, but on the inside it's a "living hell" for them. They are unable to snap out of it and pull themselves out of the valley of despair. They remind me of the woman who suffered with an infirmity for 18 years in Luke 11. The Bible, in verse 13, says she was bowed down and could *in no wise, lift herself up.*

The good news is that there is a lifting for you! There is healing for ANYONE suffering from emotional pain!

God truly can give power to you who are faint and to you who have no might, He can increase your strength (Isaiah 40:29)! Undoubtedly, your healing can be found in looking to the One who is the author and finisher of your faith (Hebrews 12:2). It can be found in looking to the One who came to heal the broken hearted, give deliverance to the captive and set at liberty them that are bruised (Luke 4:18). It can be found in looking to the One who bore all of your sorrows and weaknesses (Isaiah 53:4) at Calvary.

You may be hurting deeply right now, unable to rise above your past. It may be even difficult for you to see that Jesus loves you right where you are at. Or even more difficult to accept that no matter what you have gone through, God is able to deliver you! But the fact of the matter is, regardless to what you think, how you feel or what you say; God loves you and is able to deliver you! Not only is He able, but He's also willing. He takes delight in seeing you totally free from all emotional chains.

Just take a look at the following scriptures about God's delivering power. The Bible is always right! What it says God can do, you can be sure of it!

1. *He healeth the broken in heart, and bindeth up their wounds.* Psalm 147:3
2. *The Lord knoweth how to deliver the godly out of temptations, and to reserve the unjust unto the day of judgment to be punished.* 2 Peter 2:9
3. *Now unto him that is able to keep you from falling, and to present you faultless before the presence of his glory with exceeding joy.* Jude 1:24

4. *Behold, I am the Lord, the God of all flesh, is there anything too hard for me?* Jeremiah 32:27
5. *The Lord upholdeth all that fall, and raiseth up all those that be bowed down.* Psalm 145:14
6. *The Lord is nigh unto them that are of a broken heart; and saveth such as be of a contrite spirit.* Psalm 34:18
7. *He giveth power to the faint: and to them that have no might he increaseth strength.* Isaiah 40:29
8. *Call unto me, and I will answer thee, and shew thee great and mighty things, which thou knowest not.* Jeremiah 33:3
9. *Come unto me, all ye that labour and are heavy laden, and I will give you rest. Take my yoke upon you, and learn of me: for I am meek and lowly in heart: and ye shall find rest unto your souls. For my yoke is easy, and my burden is light.* Matthew 11:28-30.
10. *Blessed are they that mourn: for they shall be comforted* (Matthew 5:4).

Chapter 5

Unwrapping the Mummy Layers:
First Things First

Let me ask you a question, "Are you on the winning side?" By that I mean, are you a born again believer? Being a Christian, has it privileges! Romans 8:16-17 says, *The Spirit itself beareth witness with our spirit; that we are the children of God: And if children, then heirs; heirs of God, and joint-heirs with Christ...* Being an heir of God and joint-heir with Christ, grants us access to all that Jesus is and all that He has to offer us – healing, deliverance, freedom, peace, joy, love, victory and the list goes on. This is not to say that He will withhold these things from us if we are not born again. Even the bible says, in Matthew 5:45...*for he maketh his sun to rise on the evil and the good, and sendeth rain on the just and the unjust.* But as children of God, we are certainly entitled to His promises and can lay claim on any one of them. Ephesians 1:3 states, *Blessed be the God and Father of our Lord Jesus Christ, who hath blessed us with all spiritual blessings in heavenly places in Christ.*

Being a Christian also means, we are no longer enemies of God, but friends and followers of His. Whereas we once walked in darkness and walked contrary to God and everything He represents, we are now walking in oneness with God. Colossians 1:21 says, *And you, that were sometimes alienated and enemies in your mind by wicked works, yet now hath he reconciled.*

Thirdly, being a Christian means that we have hope after this world. Hope of living in a far better place than this, where there is no more emotional hurting, no more pain, no more distress; no more suffering, sickness or disease; where the streets are paved with gold, where Jesus will wipe every tear from our eyes (Revelation 21:4, 21). Indeed, being a Christian means we have everlasting life through Jesus Christ (John 3:16).

The great thing about becoming Christian is that there is absolutely nothing you have to do; no action you have to take; only BELIEVE. That's right! You don't have to make yourself right. Get yourself right. Clean yourself up or anything like that. Just simply believe. When I was on the witnessing team at my church, the people's responses when asked if they wanted to become a Christian, would always amaze me. They would say something like "I need to stop smoking first." "I'm not ready yet. I'm still caught up in doing this or doing that." "I need to get myself right first." My dear brother or sister, if we could get ourselves "right," then we would not need Jesus. The Bible clearly lets us know that there is nothing we have to do to earn salvation. Ephesians 2:8-9 says, *For by grace are ye saved through faith; and that not of yourselves; it is the gift of God. Not of works, lest any man should boast.*

If you are not saved and want to give Jesus your life today, then adhere to the following.

Romans 10:9-10 says, *That if thou shalt confess with thy mouth the Lord Jesus, and shalt believe in thine heart that God hath raised him from the dead, thou shalt be saved. For with the heart man believeth unto righteousness, and with the mouth confession is made unto salvation.* Thus salvation is easy as A, B, C to receive right now.

> A – **Admit** that you are a sinner; that you have lived contrary to God, but are now ready to repent and turn to God.
> B – **Believe** that He is the Son of God; that He died for you; but God raised Him from the dead.
> C – **Confess** that He is Lord. It is that simple!

Pray this Prayer with me:

Jesus, I ask you to forgive me of all my sins and unrighteousness. I want to know You as my Lord and Savior. I ask you to cleanse me from the filth of the world and wash me clean. I believe that You are God's son and that God raised You from the dead. Come into my heart right now, Lord. I receive your forgiveness and receive you as my Lord and Savior. Thank you for saving me! In Jesus name I pray, Amen.

Now, according to God's word (Romans 10:9-10), you are saved! You are now a born-again believer! Heaven is now rejoicing over you (Luke 15:7). Pray to God and ask Him to help you find a church where you can grow and gain spiritual strength as a new believer; a church where you can not only be a member, but be an active member, participating and fellowshipping with other like-minded saints (Proverbs 3:5-6; Hebrew 10:25).

Chapter 6

Unwrapping the Mummy Layers: The Love of God

I also mentioned in the introduction that some individuals suffering with emotional damage do not believe that God loves them, which is a very important key to their deliverance. No matter how you try to convince them otherwise, some simply see themselves as unloveable. Surely God can't love them, they think, because they are dirty. They have been violated. They are wretched. They haven't been living for Him. Their erroneous views affect their ability to love God, love others and accept God's unconditional love.

Knowing God loves you and is not upset with you or trying to punish you is a crucial step in your deliverance.

God loves you and I so much that He allowed the only Son that He had to die for us that we may have everlasting life (John 3:16). Romans 5:8 says it this way,

But God commendeth his love toward us, in that, while we were yet sinners, Christ died for us.

Now that's love! You who are parents can see that that is a strong love! To give up the only child that you have, in order that someone else's child may live eternally. If God's love for us is that strong, then His love for us certainly does not want to see us hurt or suffer. It hurts Him to see us hurt. It pains Him to see us cry. It grieves Him to see that we are unable to enjoy life because of what happened to us.

Thus, if you are to receive the healing that you need, you must KNOW that God loves you AND accepts you just as you are. Ephesians 3:17-18 says, *That Christ may dwell in your hearts by faith; that ye, being rooted and grounded in love, may be able to comprehend with all saints, what is the breadth, and length, and depth, and height: and to know the love of Christ, which passeth knowledge...* Ephesians 1:6 says, *To the praise of the glory of his grace, wherein he hath made us accepted in the beloved."* Yes, you are accepted by Christ in spite of your past, in spite of your failures, in spite of your feelings of insecurity.

God doesn't judge you based on what happened to you. He doesn't hold your past against you, but He loves you unconditionally and desires to see you whole. His love for us causes Him to also graciously extend His forgiveness to all who will receive it. His word says in Isaiah 1:18 *Come now, let us reason together, saith the Lord. Though your sins are as scarlet, they shall be as white as snow. Though they be red like crimson, I will make them white as wool.* The Lord also says in Isaiah 43:25, *I, even, I am he that blotteth out thy transgressions*

47

for mine own sake, and will not remember thy sins. Of course, His work of forgiveness is also found throughout the New Testament. The Apostle Paul writes in Ephesians 1:7, *In him we have redemption through his blood, the forgiveness of sin, in accordance with the richness of his grace.* Matthew 26:28 says, *This is my blood of the covenant, which is poured out for many for the forgiveness of sins.* With all of what God says about His forgiveness in the Bible, it is no reason to believe that He doesn't love you or holds any unforgiveness toward you.

Many times the self-worth issues that emotionally wounded individuals deal with hinder them from receiving the love God and others offer. Some have been talked down to so badly and for so long, that they feel that they are unworthy of God's love or anyone else's love for that matter. It's difficult for them to imagine that the thoughts God has toward them are good, not of evil, to give them an expected end (Jeremiah 29:11). It's difficult for them to believe that *no good thing will He withhold from them that walk uprightly* (Psalm 84:11).

Some also are unable to accept God's love because they blame Him for first allowing the malicious act to happen, then allowing it to continue to happen. They feel that if God is such a loving and just God then what happened would have never happened. Certainly it would not have happened more than once.

However, rather than blame God, you must know that God is the source of love, not pain (1 John 4:8). He is the source of healing, not hurt (Exodus 15:26). He is the solution to your problem, not the source (Philippians 4:6). While we don't understand why He allows certain things to happen, we must ask Him to help us trust Him to bring us out on victory side when they do happen.

Some emotionally bruised individuals even believe that God is angry with them – angry for not trusting Him enough for deliverance; angry that they haven't removed themselves from the situation; angry at them for the mistakes they have made. Their anger prohibits them from receiving the love that God freely provides.

Others are also angry with themselves for what happened, which makes them feel unworthy of God's love and the love of others as well. Here I must interject that even if you are angry with yourself for placing yourself in a position where you would be harmed, please let go of the anger and forgive yourself. You can't erase what has happened; however, you can learn from your mistakes. Realize that none of us are perfect. Even the bible says that all have sinned and fallen short of the glory of God (Romans 3:23).

Loving yourself helps you to love God and others.

Then some treat God as they do others. That if they are good enough or do enough good things, they can earn His love. What they fail to realize, is that all of us fall short in "doing good." We are setting ourselves up for disappointment if that is our only measure of God's love. Besides, the Bible let's us know that we <u>DO NOT</u> have to earn God's love. He gives it to us freely. Every stripe He took while hanging on the cross, the piercing of His sides and the crown of thorns placed on His head, all for you and I who did nothing to merit His actions, demonstrate God's profound love for us (Isaiah 53:5). The love God offers is truly without any strings attached. You don't have to work for it. You don't have to be "Ms. Goody this" or "Mr. Goody that." Or "Ms. Perfect this" or "Mr. Perfect that." He loves you UNCONDITIONALLY.

As I said earlier, He loves us so much that He allowed the only Son that He had to die for our sins. He didn't have to do it, but did it anyway. If we're not able to receive God's love, then we won't be able to receive the forgiveness, hope, restoration, peace and deliverance He offers.

To help you see yourself as loveable, then you should know all the wonderful things God think and says about you in His word! Surely, if God think and says good things about you, then you can too. First, He says that He created you in His own image (Genesis 1:27). Can you imagine that! You are made in the very image or likeness of God. God also says that everything that He made was very good (Genesis 1:31)! How dare you look as yourself as a bad or unloveable person, God refers to you as "very good." The bible also says in Psalm 139:14 that you are fearfully and wonderfully made. You are no mistake. God took great thought and care in creating you. It also says that you are chosen, royal and holy (1 Peter 2:9). Stop putting yourself down, God doesn't! In His eyesight, you are worthy, loveable and beautiful.

Without a doubt, knowing that you are loveable and that God loves you is a crucial key to receiving the inner healing that you long for. When you know that God loves you, you can accept His forgiveness. You can trust Him to do what's best for you. When you trust Him, you can find comfort in knowing that He will use every terrible thing that has happened to you for your good. If He died for you, then surely He doesn't mind healing your wounded soul.

He that spared not his own Son, but delivered him up for us all, how shall he not with him also freely give us all things? Romans 8:43

How do you feel about the statement, "God loves you?"

_____
_____
_____
_____
_____

_____

_____

_____

_____

_____

_____

_____

_____

_____

_____

If you are angry with God because of what
happened to you, what are some steps that you
can take now to help unload your anger?

_____

_____

_____

_____

_____

_____

_____

_____

_____

_____

_____

_____

_____

_____

_____

What steps will you commit to begin taking NOW?

_____

_____

_____

_____

_____

_____

_____

_____

_____

_____

_____

_____

_____

_____

Try this simple exercise.

Write down how you feel when angry and resentful thoughts come to your mind about God?

_____

_____

_____

_____

_____

_____

_____

_____

_____

_____

_____

Now write down how you feel when you good and positive thoughts about God. Even if you are angry with God for whatever reason, there is still something good that can be said about Him.

_____
_____
_____
_____
_____
_____
_____
_____
_____
_____

Compare your feelings. Which makes you feel better, lighter, peaceful, less stressed? Which strengthens your faith?

_____
_____
_____
_____
_____
_____
_____
_____
_____
_____
_____
_____
_____

Chapter 7

Unwrapping the Mummy Layers: Healing Belongs to You

I mentioned earlier in this book that some emotionally wounded individuals are unable to receive God's healing power because they don't believe that healing belongs to them. While some want to be healed, they think that healing belongs to everyone except them. The unfortunate things that they have experienced have beaten them down so badly that they can't phantom anything good happening to them. They feel unworthy and undeserving. But if you desire to be made whole by Christ, then you must know, accept and believe that healing belongs to you as God's child. Yes it most certainly does!

The Lord said in His word in Exodus 15:26 that *I am the Lord that healeth thee.* Well who is thee? Thee includes you and thee includes me. In Isaiah 53:5, the word of God says....*and with his stripes we are healed.* Well, who are we? We, again includes you and it includes me. There's no where in the bible that says because you are an emotionally wounded person that you cannot be healed. There's no where in the bible that says because you failed to remove yourself from the situation that God isn't going to heal you. Indeed, there's no where in the bible that says because what happened was your fault, God won't help you. As a matter of fact, we find in the bible, in the book of Judges, that in many instances the children of Israel caused many calamities to come their way. Yet, God extended His mercy to them each and every time and delivered them from their oppressors. As Psalm 103:8 says, *The Lord is merciful and gracious, slow to anger, plenteous in mercy.*

There's just simply no where in the Bible that states that healing is for a select group of people. But from the beginning to the end, the Bible lets us know that healing is for everyone, for anyone who believes and claims this precious promise. Our God has no respect of persons (Romans 2:11). Healing is for YOU! It is not His will that you be tormented in your mind, spirit or your soul in any kind of way. Psalm 23:3 let's you know that God delights to grant you peace and restore your soul (Psalm 23:1-3).

So again I say, that if you want to be healed of your emotional wounds, KNOW that God's promise of healing belongs to YOU. Healing is God's children bread (Mark 7:25-29).

What do you think about the statement that inner healing belongs to all God's children?

_____

_____

_____

_____

_____

_____
_____
_____
_____

Are there any misconceptions (false beliefs) that
you have about God's promise to heal His
children? _____ Some may have been taught
to you as a child. Others may have been told to
you by someone you trusted or looked up too. If
so, list them here.

_____
_____
_____
_____
_____
_____
_____
_____
_____
_____

What does the Bible say about each
misconception you listed?

_____
_____
_____
_____
_____
_____
_____

_____

_____

_____

_____

_____

_____

_____

_____

_____

_____

_____

_____

Choose this day to believe the report of the Lord!

Isaiah 53:1 Who hath believed our report? And to whom is the arm of the Lord revealed?

Chapter 8

Unwrapping the Mummy Layers:
How bad do you want it?

Are you sick and tired of being sick and tired? Usually deliverance for any individual depends on how bad they want it. Are you really tired of thinking or dreaming about living your life to the fullest? Are you really ready to be delivered from fear, anger, pretense and other mummy layers? Or are you just saying you are tired of being bound?

When we want something bad enough, we do what it takes to get it!

This reminds me of a movie written by Tyler Perry entitled *Madea's Family Reunion*. The movie evolves around a young woman who is in a physically and mentally abusive relationship with a young man. He is very successful and can offer her the finest things in life. What made matters worse for this young woman is that when she turned to her own mother for help, the mother blamed the young woman for her mistreatment, telling her that she must have said something or did something to anger the young man and cause him to beat her.

Well, the young lady was pushed and pushed so until one day, she had enough! She not only fought back, but she found the strength to leave this young man for good. Not even the plush lifestyle that he offered, appealed to her anymore. She reached the point where she was sick and tired of being sick and tired. So again I say, when we want something bad enough, we not only say we want to move forward, but we actually move forward.

Remember again the question that Jesus asked the man at the pool of Bethseda? Jesus asked him, *"Wilt thou be made whole?"* Jesus knew He had the ability to heal the man. He knew He was willing to heal the man. He knew that the man was in a terrible condition and that the man had been this way for a long time. BUT, He first wanted to know if the man wanted to be healed bad enough, bad enough to believe and take action.

Ponder that question here for a few moments. Really think about it. Do you really want to be made whole? Are you sick and tired of suffering? Are you ready to take action? As I mentioned earlier in this book, many have dealt with their predicament for so long that they have accepted it as a way of life. To them life, is being an emotional prisoner. They are functioning, but they are not free. They have learned to live with it.

However, if you really want inner healing, then I admonish you today to choose life over destruction; healing over pain; joy over sorrow. Choose to do something about your condition.

Yes it is easier to do nothing, after all doing nothing requires no effort. It is easier to remain as you are. You don't have to leave your comfort zone.

Even when you make the decision to take charge of your life, a tug of war within can break out. A part of you really wants to let go of what happened to you, but the other part of you finds it difficult to forget the bad thing that was done or said to you. A part of you really wants to let go, but the other part wants them to pay for what they have done. That part feels that to let the hurt go, means the other person is getting off too easy. You are sort of in the predicament that the Apostle Paul found himself in, in Romans 7:19. Paul says, *For the good that I would I do not: but the evil which I would not, that I do.*

However, you must want your healing bad enough to do whatever it takes "in righteousness" to receive it. Yes, in righteousness. Our hurt can cause us so much pain, that the anger we feel can send us into a rage to "settle the score" in an ungodly way with the person who wronged us.

My dear brother, my dear sister, know that God really does want to free you! Part of you taking action involves you owning up to what you feel and the damage it has caused you (We will discuss this more in the next chapter). No more pretending. No more hiding. No more blaming others or blaming God. Ask God to help you give your emotional pain to Him. Make up in your mind today to take action. To follow the directives God gives you; to follow the advice of others God has placed in your life to help you. No, you won't forget the event, but you can receive healing for it so that you are no longer held captive by it.

Here's where committing to a plan of action comes to play. As you will notice, I have given you space in various chapters to write your thoughts, your feelings, and things you plan to do to help you recover from your past or present experiences. An action plan will help you put things into proper perspective and help you move forward in the right direction.

Committing to a plan of action will not be easy. It will be much easier for you to stay as you are, with what you are comfortable with. After all, who wants to revisit the hurt that has caused them to be in the state they are in, in the first place? But as painful as it may be, your efforts will be well worth the results and benefits that you will receive - benefits of wholeness, peace and rest in your mind, spirit and soul, to name a few. All of these can be more than wishful thinking. With God's help, they can become a reality for you.

It will hurt to revisit the pain.

You will be disgusted, frustrated and disappointed at times during your healing process. You may even want to give up because the pain and hurt you are encountering seems too much to bear. But again, the wholeness you shall receive will be well worth it.

Start off taking small steps. Remember depending on the depth and nature of your emotional wound, healing will take time. Perhaps it could be simply talking to a trusted friend about what you are dealing with. Think about how much better we often feel after we share with another what's going on with us. James 5:16 says, *Confess your faults one to another, and pray one for another, that ye may be healed...*

You've held it in long enough. Now it is time to release it to someone you trust, someone who has your best interest at heart. Talking about your issues can also give you a release from pent up negative emotions and help bring your real issues into focus.

Another small step can involve you daily reading scriptures about God's love, His forgiveness and His delivering power. God's word is like a balm in Gilead. It's like medicine to our wounded souls. In times of despair, try reading in the book of Psalms. The book of Psalms contains many comforting scriptures relating to distress. Then you can write in a journal your thoughts and feelings about what you read. Writing can also help you put things into proper perspective.

Perhaps becoming involved in a support group or calling a support hotline established to help those dealing with a similar issue will be something you are willing to do. Utilizing a support hotline can grant you the anonymity you may desire at this point.

Whatever step you choose to take, just take it. Remember faith without works is dead (James 2:17).

Taking action also involves you taking control over your thoughts or the thoughts you choose to entertain in your mind. Are your thoughts focused on your wound or the wound healer? Are your thoughts focused on what happened to you; on what you may or may not have done to cause this to happen to you? Or are your thoughts focused on casting your cares upon Jesus, knowing that He cares for you (1 Peter 5:7)! Are your thoughts focused on your anger, your fear, your depression, your desire to retaliate or focused on getting the help you need to free you from these negative layers?

Sometimes we allow our minds to ruminate over and over and over on bad things that were done to us and said to us. This usually makes us more angry, more bitter and resentful, more depressed, and more stressed about our situations. Guy Winch in his article, *5 Tips for Recovering from Emotional Pain*, points out that there is a difference between reflecting and ruminating about a past event. He says that reflecting about your past can help you learn from your past mistakes or failures and use the experience to help someone else. On the other hand, ruminating, Winch says in his article, *5 Tips for Healing Emotional Pain,* only increases your stress levels and can be addictive. Reflecting prompts progress, but ruminating gets a person stuck. Reflecting brings about testimony, but ruminating brings about more bondage.

Hence, a key step in receiving emotional deliverance also includes guarding the thoughts that you entertain in your mind. Thinking on the wrong thoughts constantly will constantly provide you with feelings that will only eat away at you. The longer you think on them, the harder it will be to cast those thoughts down. It is best that when bad thoughts first come, to do as 2 Corinthians 10:5 instructs,

> *Casting down imaginations, and every high thing that exalteth itself against the knowledge of God, and bringing into captivity every thought to the obedience of Christ.*

This may be challenging to do, but you will find the longer you allow a negative thought to remain, the harder it will be to uproot it.

What plan are you willing to begin executing to help you walk in freedom?

Chapter 9

Unwrapping the Mummy Layers: Face the Truth

Another important key in receiving inner healing is first ADMITTING that you have a problem. I mentioned this important key in the last chapter. Denying the problem or that your hurt exist will do nothing to aid you in receiving the deliverance that you need. Denying your problem prevents God's healing virtue from flowing in your life. You will find that both Christian and secular counselors believe that that admitting there is a problem is the first step in getting help. After all, how can God help you if you are telling Him that nothing is wrong; that you are okay?

Thus if you truly want to be free, then you must come clean. Think about this. Let's say, for example, that a person breaks a leg and as a result has to go to the emergency room. Rather than saying "I broke my leg," when the doctor asks what's wrong, the person says "Nothing's wrong." Well, how can the doctor provide needed medical assistance to a problem that "doesn't exist?" Likewise, Doctor Jesus can not provide the healing you need, if you deny your problem exist. Moreover, denying your problem will not only eat you up on the inside, but it will also negatively affect other areas of your life – how you relate and respond to others; your feelings about things, how you view things, etc.

I know that for many of you denial is the shield that protects you from painful memories of the past. For many of you, just to think about what happened causes a hurt that you really want to forget. It causes you to relive all the negativity and ugliness that you experienced. In addition, it can involve embarrassment issues for you, your family, and the person who did it, especially if they hold a key position in the church or society. You may even feel that if you come clean, no one will believe you anyway or that others will take the perpetuator's word over yours.

If admittance is a problem area for you, then I admonish you to cry out to God and ask the Savior to help you face your problem. He has promised that if we cry out to Him, He will help us. Psalm 18:6 says, *In my distress I called upon the Lord, and cried unto my God: he heard my voice out of his temple, and my cry came before him, even into his ears.*

Are you in any way distressed today?

Oh there are many verses in the bible (Psalm 34:6; Psalm 34:17; Psalm 55:16; Psalm 61:2 *Psalm 77:1)* that tell us that not only does God hear us when we cry out to Him, but He answers. Thus, if admitting your problem is a troublesome area for you, then cry out to God and He will help you. Of course, none of us want to look back or even think about the hurtful things said or done to us in the past. However most, if not all of us, will admit that we don't like the bondage it has created for us either.

Again, I will acknowledge that admitting one has a problem is easier said than done. But, it MUST be done. Yes, it's true that God already knows what happened. He is omniscient (all knowing). The Psalmist said in Psalm 139:2-4,

> *Thou knowest my downsitting and mine uprising, thou understandest my thought, afar off. Thou compassest my path and my lying down, and art acquainted with all thy ways. For there is not a word in my tongue, but, lo, O Lord, thou knowest it altogether.*

God knows everything, but He wants you to be real with Him. Just like the woman did with the issue of blood (Matthew 9:20-22; Mark 5:25-34; Luke 8:43-48). She didn't allow the ugliness of her issue cause her to hide herself and pretend like everything was okay. She didn't allow what others said or thought about her keep her behind closed doors. Nor did she allow the stink of her situation cause her to lose hope and faith.

Has your suffering caused you to lose faith? Confidence?

In spite of the gossips in town and the naysayers, this woman sought out Jesus. When she found Him, she came clean with Him! In public view, she reached out to Christ and guess what? Christ reached back out to her! He knew the seriousness of her condition. He knew she had suffered for a very long time (12 years). He even knew others were probably calling her nasty names and shunned her from their company, and by law she shouldn't have been in public. Nevertheless, once the woman touched the hem of His garment, He made her whole! Glory! Christ made her whole! Let me interject here that Christ wholeness is not only for women. But it's everyone - for men, children, teenagers, young adults, whoever needs His healing touch (Acts 10:38)!

I admonish you to stop pretending like that situation did not happen. Even more so, stop pretending like it didn't affect you. Tell God all about it.

God sees. He knows, and He cares.

Why do you feel it is necessary to pretend that nothing happened to you? (if this is the case with you)

_____

_____

_____

_____

_____

_____

_____

_____

_____

_____

_____

_____

_____

_____

_____

_____

_____

Now from what you just listed, which one can God not help you overcome?

_____

_____

_____

_____

_____

_____

_____

_____

_____

_____

_____

_____

_____

Will you being to trust Him today?

Chapter 10

Unwrapping the Mummy Layers:

UnForgiveness

I purposely chose to write an entire chapter dealing with unforgiveness for it is something that will surely block God's healing virtue in our lives. I mentioned it to some extent in the chapter dealing with mummy layers, but so critical is its role in receiving inner healing, I felt it necessary to write a chapter discussing it.

We are all tempted to act in an unforgiving manner toward those who have hurt us. Certainly, when we are hurt, we want to hurt back. As Jesus said in His word, ...*The Spirit indeed is willing, but the flesh is weak* (Matthew 26:41). Rather than forgive, sometimes our hurt causes us to want to retaliate to the point that our thoughts are consumed with how and what we can do to get back at those who have offended us. What a burden that is to carry around! How miserable that makes us feel!

However, forgiveness releases us from carrying that heavy burden, and it is ESSENTIAL if you are going to receive the inner healing you need from God. The temptation to take matters into your own hands, to seek revenge, to not forgive, will always present itself. But we must remember that God says

Vengeance is mine; I will repay, (Romans 12:19). Vengeance, most certainly is God's business.

Consider Jesus. He had every reason to be angry and unforgiving toward those who wronged Him – the Pharisees, the scribes, the Sadducees; those who scourged Him; those who betrayed Him; those who lied on Him; those who tried to trick Him, and those who denied Him. Yet while on the cross, He tells His father, regarding those who were responsible for his crucifixion, *Father, forgive them: for they know not what they do (Luke 23:34).* You may say, "Well, I am not Jesus." Yes, that is true. But as a born again believer, you have the Spirit of Christ living on the inside of you which helps you to walk in the same forgiveness as Jesus did, if you allow it.

Forgiving others is a choice.

Think about that. It is a choice. It is not something that you will automatically do when wronged. It is not something you will feel like doing when wronged. As a matter of fact, if you are waiting until you "feel like it" before you forgive others, then you will probably be in for a long, long wait. Nevertheless, forgiving others is something you must choose to do if you want to experience God's healing for your soul.

You have the choice of choosing to cast your burden on God and forgive or hold on to the hurt, bitterness and pain.

I'm here to tell you that holding on to unforgiveness will only eat away at you, but it will also intensify the bitterness, resentment, and depression that you already feel. Unforgiveness also gives place to the enemy to continue to wreck havoc in your life. 2 Corinthians 2:10-11 says, *To whom ye forgive any thing, I forgive also; for if I forgave any thing, to whom I forgave it, for your sakes forgave I it in the person of Christ; Lest Satan should get an advantage of us: for we are not ignorant of his devices.* We must trust God to make things right. When we forgive, God can do just that.

Unforgiveness not only hinders you from receiving God's healing, but it can affect your physical health as well. Pent up emotions such anger, resentment and bitterness that result from unforgiveness, can contribute to the development of ulcers, high blood and other physical problems if not properly handled. Just think about how you feel in moments of anger. Sometimes, it may feel as if you are about to pop a blood vessel. Your heart beat becomes rapid. Sometimes it becomes difficult for you to breathe. Indeed, unforgiveness can be potentially damaging to you physically.

So importance is forgiveness that the Lord included it in His prayer *"And forgive us our debts, as we forgive our* debtors (Matthew 6:12). He knew the important role of forgiveness in our relationship with others. He also says if we don't forgive, neither will God forgive us, *And when you stand praying, forgive, if ye have ought against any: that you Father also which is in heaven m ay forgive you your trespasses. But if ye do not forgive, neither will your Father which is in heaven forgive your trespasses* (Mark 11:25-26).

Without a doubt, forgiveness releases us to get help for our souls. It releases us to go on with life. It releases us to love others; to open up to others; to bless and pray for others, even our enemies (Luke 6:27-28). Forgiveness doesn't mean that we are acknowledging that what happened to us wasn't a bad thing, quite the contrary. Forgiveness is acknowledging that what happen to us was bad, yet we are choosing to turn the situation over to God for Him to handle. Forgiveness blesses you more than you realize.

You are helping yourself the most when you forgive and hurting yourself the most when you don't.

I'm reminded of another movie by Tyler Perry, entitled *Diary of a Mad Black Woman.* The black woman in this story endured much mistreatment from her successful, yet egotistical husband. He lied to her. He talked down to her. He cheated. Finally, one day he put her out of the home they shared in front of his mistress. Talk about embarrassing! She had no place to go and nothing to fall back on. She had access to none of their money and the house was in his name. As expected, this woman was very hurt, disgraced, betrayed, and denied everything that she had helped her husband acquire. The person she loved with all her heart did not loved her. As a matter of fact he loathed her. He treated her with such contempt. She was nothing in his eyes.

Well one day, the chips turned. This highly successful attorney was shot in the courtroom after failing to help a dishonest client get off the hook. As a result, he was paralyzed. What did this woman do? She moved back in with her husband in order to provide him with much needed physical assistance. She did right by a person who did no right by her.

Are you able to do right by those who have wronged you?

What did she get in return? He continued to talk down to her and degrade her. Now that's a real test! This sent this woman into a rage, causing her to get even with him in as many ways as she could think of. But, one day her mom talked to her about forgiveness. Her mom told her that although her husband had hurt her real bad, that she must forgive him, not for him, but for her. Her mom went on to explain that when an individual hurts another individual, the person who is doing the hurt gets power over the other person. If the other person doesn't forgive the individual for what they have done, then the individual will keep that power of them. She finally told her daughter to forgive him and that after she forgives him, to forgive herself.

Is today the day for you to come to yourself and begin walking in forgiveness?

When the young lady "came to herself" and actually forgave her husband, she began dealing with him with great care and compassion, rather than rage. Indeed, she began dealing with him in accordance to God's word.

But I say unto you which hear, Love your enemies, do good to them which hate you. Bless them that curse you, and pray for them which despitefully use you. (Luke 6:27-29)

What did this do for her? In the end she was able to move on with her life, completely released from all the pain, anger, rage and hurt she had felt. She opened herself up to love again.

True forgiveness is indeed liberating!

Not only must we forgive those who have wronged us, but we must also forgive ourselves and God. Sometimes those who are emotionally wounded blame themselves and will not forgive themselves for what happened to them. This is a trick of the enemy! It wasn't your fault that your dad walked out on your family when you were a child. It wasn't your fault that a damaged person molested you at a young age. It wasn't your fault that the man you were married to thought it was better to beat you than love you. No, none of these ugly situations were your fault.

Even if you have suffered emotional damage because of mistake you made, FORGIVE yourself. Ask God to help you to stop beating yourself over the head about what happened to you. You cannot change the past. However, you can learn from it and move on. Don't allow unforgiveness and blame paralyze you, keeping you from reaching out to God, from praying to Him, from enjoying a relationship with Him. If God forgives you then you must also forgive yourself.

If we confess our sins, he is faithful and just to forgive us our sins, and to cleanse us from all unrighteousness (1 John 1:9).

Even if you feel "unclean" because of your past, this scripture lets you know that God is able and will cleanse you from all filthiness, if you turn to Him.

You must also forgive God and stop blaming Him for what happened. You may even have to ask God to help you to forgive Him and stop blaming Him, particularly if these are very difficult for you to do. See, sometimes the pain of our suffering is so great and hard to bear, that we become very, very angry. This is the case particularly when the loss we experience seems unjust and surreal. Consider the parents of an infant child who suddenly dies of natural causes or from an unfortunate event at the age of 2, not even having the time to enjoy life at all. An event like this can cause the parents of this young infant to blame God as they struggle to understand why He allowed such a tragedy to happen. As you can imagine, situations like these require much, much prayer, empathy and time in order to help heal the hurting parents.

Although we question God as to why bad things happen to us, we must pray at these times that God grant us the strength to accept what happened, the strength to trust Him, and the strength to reach out to Him rather than blame withdraw from Him.

Some things we will never completely understand. 1 Corinthians 12:9 says, for *we know in part....* But one thing is for certain and that is God is our heavenly Father and we are His children. As with any good parent, He doesn't desire to hurt us. He doesn't desire to do us harm. But, He desires to bless us and take the very best care of us.

Rather than being angry at God, know that He has the ability to work ALL things out, regardless to how cruel and hurtful they are, for your good. Romans 8:28 states, *And we know that all things work together for the good, to them who love God, to them who are the called according to His purpose.* Satan and the one who wronged you may have meant it for your bad; but God can use it for your good!

Just take a look at Joseph's story beginning in Genesis, chapter 37. The bible says that Joseph's father, Jacob, loved Joseph more than all his brothers and made him a coat of many colors. This caused his own brothers to envy and hate him. On top of this, Joseph had a dream that one day he would rule over his entire family. Boy, did this upset his brothers! They were so caught up in anger, envy and jealousy that they devised a plan to kill him (I told you earlier that emotions out of control can cause a person to commit a crime).

However, one of his brothers, Reuben, decided that this was not the best thing to do. He talked his brothers into throwing Joseph into a waterless pit, thinking that he would later rescue Joseph. However, his brother Judah, concerned about bearing the guilt of Joseph's death, suggested to his brothers, in verse 26, that they sell Joseph into slavery to the Ishmeelites. How cruel! How cold and callous! They were not at all concerned about what would happen to Joseph, whether he lived or died, or how Joseph would be treated in slavery. They simply didn't want his blood to be upon their hands. They probably thought they would never see Joseph again.

So they sold Joseph into slavery. The bible then says in verse 31 that they took action to cover up their misdeed. Isn't that much like your oppressor? Always trying to cover up the bad things they have done to you and against you. But the bible says in Luke 12:2 *for that is nothing covered, that shall not be revealed; neither hid, that shall not be known.* Joseph's brother killed an animal and dipped the coat they had stripped from him into the animal's blood. Then they lied to their father saying (in verse 32) that they found Joseph's coat, but did not know what happened to him. Our oppressors even try to cover up their bad deeds with one lie after another. Yet, God sees everything. Indeed, His eyes are in every place beholding the good and the evil (Proverbs 15:3).

The story goes on to let us know that while in slavery, Joseph experienced one event after another. He was falsely accused of rape and as a result thrown in jail. All of the bad things that happened to him were no fault of his own, but all began with the malicious deeds of his brother.

Have the unfortunate things that have happened to you been due to no fault of your own? Take comfort in knowing that you are not alone in this type of suffering.

To make a long story short, later in the book of Genesis (chapters 42-44) Joseph's brothers had to travel to the land where he lived in order to get food due to a famine in their homeland. Joseph at first disguises himself from them. He later reveals himself in chapter 45, and then makes a very moving statement to his brothers in chapter 50:20. Joseph says,

But as for you (meaning his brothers), ye thought evil against me: but God meant it unto good, to bring to pass, as it is this day, to save much people alive.

Be encouraged to know that your story involves a bigger plan for you! It is far more than the hurt, betrayal, pain and anger that you feel. God has something glorious in mind for you! Your pain is not the end of your story. Your suffering is not for naught! The Apostle Paul says it best in Romans 8:18,

For I reckon that the sufferings of this present time are not worthy to be compared with the glory which shall be revealed in us.

Talking about forgiveness! Joseph's own blood brothers devised and carry out a plot against him. Joseph lost many years of his youth and spent many years as a slave because of their callous actions.

Have you spent many years as a "slave" to your emotions as a result of the callous actions of others?

Yet, when given the opportunity to retaliate, He CHOSE to forgive and love. He didn't hold malice, resentment or bitterness in his heart against them or God, releasing himself to move forward in life and reach his God-given destiny! Of a surety, forgiveness releases you to move on to your purpose and destiny in life!

You may ask, "If I forgive, will I be totally released from the anger, the hurt that I feel?" I would say, for some of you, you will. For others, you may feel a trace of the hurt and anger from time to time when you encounter that person, but that doesn't mean that you haven't forgiven. During one of my teleconferences, we discussed the subject of emotional healing. One of the participants shared how she was raped by someone in her family during her childhood. Although she didn't understand why it happened to her, she gave praise to God as she discussed how He healed her completely from this violent act. She stated that with God's help, she was able to forgive the family member who did this to her and felt no anger, bitterness or resentment towards him. She admitted that she tried with everything in her to be angry at him for what He had done, but God did not allow her to do so.

Another participant shared how she was in an abusive marriage, and although she had forgiven her husband for what he had done, sometimes thinking about the event from time to time would rekindle anger and bitterness in her. Sometimes when she saw him, these feelings would rise up as well. When asked if she acted upon any of these feelings, she responded, "No." I truly believe this young woman had forgiven her husband and told her to be encouraged that in the process of time, God would even heal her completely of those feelings. Sometimes individuals beat themselves up because they believe that since they have forgiven, then they shouldn't feel any remorse, anger or bitterness toward the person who wronged them. While God can completely heal a person from these feelings, He can also help us to walk in forgiveness toward our debtors even while freeing us completely from the feelings we are leaving behind.

What decision will you make that will help you to forgive those who have wronged you?

_____

_____

_____

_____

_____

_____

_____

_____

_____

_____

_____

_____

_____

_____

_____

Chapter 11

Unwrapping the Mummy Layers: Unfailing Faith

I believe the story of Jesus, Martha, Mary and Lazarus in John 11 contains many other truths that can further help unwrap you from the mummy layers in your life. In particular, their story demonstrates the type of faith needed to get inner healing.

The story begins by telling us that Lazarus was sick. This prompted his sisters, Mary and Martha, to send for Jesus. Jesus, once getting the news, responded by saying in verse 4,...*This sickness is not unto death, but for the glory of God that the Son of God might be glorified thereby."* Here is the first glimpse of good news for you. Perhaps the emotional damaged you have incurred has imprisoned you to the point that you feel dead – spiritually, emotionally, mentally and physically. You may have even asked yourself is life worth living. My dear brother or dear sister, take great comfort in knowing that your years of abuse, turmoil, hurt, embarrassment and discomfort is not unto death. You may feel dead, but what you went through will not take you under. God is able to restore and revive you! Just as Ezekiel prophesied to the dry, lifeless bones in Ezekiel

37, God is able to prophesy to you and bring you back to life!

The story goes on to tell us about Jesus' love for Martha, Mary and Lazarus. Verse 5 says, *"Now Jesus loved Martha, and her sister, and Lazarus."* His love for them prompted Him to come and see about His friends, just like it would any of us. Verse 6 tells us that instead of Jesus rushing to see Lazarus when He got the news, He delayed His coming for two days. It seemed like an urgent situation since John's sister took the time to send for Him. Let's say, for example, had it been something like a cold or if Lazarus had hurt himself while working, then it would not have been necessary to send for Jesus. But the fact that Lazarus' sisters took the time to send for Him, indicates that it was an emergent situation. Yet, Jesus remained where He was for two days. Surely, with Jesus being omniscient (all knowing), He knew exactly what was going on with Lazarus. Surely, He knew the urgency of the situation. Surely!

Have you ever felt that Jesus delayed His answer to you, although you prayed and told Him about the urgency of the situation?

Perhaps, you have been praying and praying, reaching out to Jesus for Him to deliver you, yet it seems if your prayer requests have fallen on deaf ears. Be encouraged to know that Jesus' silence does not mean He has not heard you. It has often been said that, "Delayed does not mean denied."

Remember the story of the Syrophenician woman in Matthew 15:21-28? This non-Jewish woman asked Jesus to come and heal her daughter. When she first asked, Jesus said not a word. It was if He was ignoring her. On top of that, His disciples wanted Him to send her away because she was getting on their nerves. Then on top of that, when Jesus finally responds to her, He said something that really challenged her faith. He said in verse 24, *I am not sent but unto the lost sheep of the house of Israel.* In other words, Jesus told the woman that His ministry was to the Jews, not non-Jews. But this woman, being fervent in her faith, pressed on. In the face of what seemed like a negative response from Jesus, the woman held on to her faith. The end of the story let's us know that because of her faith, she got what she wanted. Her daughter was completely healed.

Your faith must press on even when it seems like Jesus is not responding to your request.

So, take comfort in knowing that just because Jesus hasn't acted right away in your situation that it doesn't mean that He is not concerned. Neither does it mean that He is not hearing your cry. Don't allow your faith to turn cold. You must know that God has Your best interest at heart. It may not seem like it, but He really does. As ugly as your situation may be, God still knows what's best and His appointed time He will act.

He's never too late, but right on time!

Let me continue with the story. So Jesus delays His coming for two days, but keep in mind, He had already said that Lazarus' sickness was not unto death, but that the glory of God may be reveal. This lets us know that God had a plan in mind for healing Lazarus. He also has a plan in mind for healing you!

Finally, Jesus decides to head to Bethany where Lazarus was. On the way, He informs His disciples that Lazarus had died. When Jesus reaches Bethany, in verse 17, He finds that Lazarus had been in the grave four whole days (but He already knew that too!). When Lazarus' sisters found out Jesus had come, Martha went to meet him, but Mary remained in the house. Oh I'm sure this was such a touching scene to see. Everyone was full of sorrow, weeping because Lazarus had died. When Martha saw Jesus, she told him that if he had have been there, Lazarus would not have died. Such was the track record of Jesus! Everyone knew He had the power to heal; to calm the raging sea; to cast out demons and to give victory over death! So she knew that if Jesus had been there, her brother would not have died.

Now take a further look at Martha's remarkable faith in God! She went on to tell Jesus that although her brother had been dead for four days, He STILL had the power to raise Him again. That even though Lazarus was dead, whatever Jesus would ask God to do, God would do it!

This is exactly the type of faith you must have in order to receive your inner healing – to believe in God against all odds; to believe in His ability to restore you although you feel you have been emotionally dead for days, weeks, months or even years; to believe in His ability to deliver no matter what or who it is you need deliverance from. You must be like Abraham who the bible says in Romans 4:18, *who against hope believed in hope, that he might become the father of many nations;* who says *calleth those things which be not as though they were* (verse 17), knowing that there is death and life in the power of the tongue (Proverbs 18:21).

Indeed, my brother and my sister, you must believe that God is able to un-wrap every mummy layer hindering you from having quality of life you desire! Our God most certainly can turn your joy into sorrow; give you hope for tomorrow; give you beauty for ashes and the oil of joy for mourning; give you the garment of praise for the spirit of heaviness: that you might be called trees of righteousness, the planting of the Lord, that he might be glorified! (Isaiah 61:3)

It will be challenging many times to hold on to your faith, especially in the face of little to no progress; especially when it seems like you are sinking further into a bottomless pit; especially when it seems like life for you is even more distressing, while life for the person who harmed you couldn't be better. Yes, on the road to recovery, the pain and hurt will resurface again. But dear heart, have faith in God – holding on faith, persevering faith, keeping on faith!

Jesus then makes a profound and very encouraging statement to Martha in verse 23. He says *"Thy brother shall rise again."* What a statement! Lazarus had been dead for four entire days; yet, Jesus tells Martha that He shall rise again. I'm sure Martha was astonished at this point, knowing that Jesus can do anything, but at the same time amazed at His statement.

Please, receive Jesus' word today. You too shall rise again! Your life isn't over! This is not the end for you! What happened to you is not the end of the story for you! You will smile again! Indeed, weeping may endure for a night, but joy is coming in the morning (Psalm 30:5)!

Martha's next statement illustrates both her astonishment and her lack of understanding of what Jesus was really saying. She tells Jesus that she knows that Lazarus will rise again in the resurrection (v. 24), oblivious to the fact that Jesus was actually telling her that He was going to raise Lazarus from the dead. Sometimes the difficult and trying situations we have experienced in life make us dull to the miraculous power of God. We know that He can deliver and that He can do anything but fail, but because of the hurt, emotional pain and suffering we have undergone we become indifferent to His miraculous power. Nevertheless, God is still able.

The rest of the story lets us know that Jesus, once taken to the place where Lazarus laid, cried with a loud voice, *Lazarus come forth.* The bible says in verse 44, *And he that was dead came forth, bound hand and foot with graveclothes: and his face was bound about with a napkin. Jesus said unto them, Loose him and let him go!* My, my, what a miraculous display of the resurrection power of our Lord! Lazarus, once bound by death, was freed by the miracle working power of God!

I don't know what your "grave clothes" may be on today; perhaps, it's an unfortunate event that happened in your childhood; perhaps, it's an abusive relationship that you can't seem to get out of; perhaps, it is fear, rejection, depression, rejection, and so forth and so on. Whatever it may be, KNOW that God has the power to loose you from it, freeing you to go forth in life and become all that He wants you to be! Glory! This reminds me of a song that my late pastor, Bishop G.E. Patterson, used to sing from time to time. The lyrics are:

I am free
Praise the Lord I'm free
No longer bound
No more chains holding me
My soul is resting
And that's another blessing
Praise the Lord, Hallelujah I'm free!

The end of the story without a doubt lets us know that Jesus demonstrated victory over death by raising Lazarus from the dead! For four days, his cold, lifeless body lay in a grave. But even the grave couldn't defeat the power of Jesus, and neither can the deadness of your situation overcome Jesus' resurrecting power! This same victorious power is available to you today! Receive it!

In what ways have your faith been challenged by your present or past?

_____
_____
_____
_____
_____
_____
_____
_____
_____
_____
_____
_____
_____
_____
_____

Do you believe that God can and is willing to help you?

_____
_____
_____

Chapter 12
Unwrapping the Mummy Layers:
Fear - The Progress Blocker

I mentioned earlier in this book that fear is one of the mummy layers holding individuals back from their deliverance. Emotionally hurt people are afraid to reach out to others, afraid to form relationship with others, and are afraid that others will find out about the "secret" they have been carrying around for years.

Well, fear is also a "progress blocker" for the emotional wounded. It keeps them in bondage, afraid to walk the road of recovery. Emotionally damaged individuals are fearful of reaching out for help, seeing themselves as defeated before they even try. They are afraid to take steps that I and others have offered to get their deliverance. Their fear of failure causes them to feel powerless and as a result some make poor choices. They are bombarded with negative thoughts such as "What's the use? It won't help." "I tried before, but I didn't get anywhere." Pessimism and gloom clouds their thinking and decisions.

Fear is a constant companion for some of them. Even if they try to move forward, fear is right there in their thoughts and ears, saying "You won't get anywhere." Fear constantly bombards them with the "what if" question. "What if this happens or what if that happens," always pointing to the worse case scenarios. To the woman who tries to leave her abuser, fear says "He'll find you. You won't be able to escape." To the child who has been molested, fear says "If you tell, you will make him or her angry. You will cause embarrassment to yourself and to your family." To the young lady who is in a codependent relationship with a female friend (I'm not talking about a homosexual life style here, but a heterosexual relationship where two woman are friends), fear says "She'll retaliate if you leave the friendship. You can't possibly be a true friend."

Fear causes constant worry and stress for the already emotionally distraught individual. It robs them of their peace and keeps their minds focused on the negative. Fear definitely keeps them in turmoil and distress. As 1John 4:18 says, …..*fear hath torment.*

Fear can imprison us to the point that it overshadows our thoughts and actions, blocking us from thinking clearly and moving on in life.

When we are fearful, our usual response is to runaway or escape. However, in order to heal from emotional wounds, an individual must ask God for the courage to face their fears so that they can move on. As one writer puts it "Your healing lies on the other side of fear." The word of God tells us in 2 Timothy 1:7, *For God hath not given us the spirit of fear, but of power, and of love, and of sound mind.* Yet the enemy works overtime to keep many of the emotionally wounded from grasping this truth. Even those who are not in deep emotional pain allow fear to rob them of moving forward in life.

Without a doubt, fear is an impediment to healing and progress. Some of us have lived with it for so long until it is comfortable for us. It's a way of life for us. It keeps us from having to push ourselves of our comfort zones. It keeps us from speaking up for ourselves. It keeps us from revisiting our pasts, our pains, our wounds, our bitterness, our unforgiveness, hindering us from progressing toward our future.

Many times we hold on to fear because to let it go means that we have to take charge; we have to take action; we have to do something different than what we have been doing. We have to think differently. We have to respond differently. Yet relinquishing our fears to Jesus will help us to begin to walk in the freedom that we so desire.

Casting all your care upon Him; for He careth for you. 1 Peter 5:7

Take a few moments. I want you to really think about what it is that's causing you to fear. If you think long enough, you can usually pinpoint it. Regardless to what it is or how many things it may be, begin one by one, relinquishing your fears to Jesus. Difficult it is, but it can be done with God's help. Ask Him to help you lay aside the weight of fear in your life. He truly is the One who can truly deliver you. The psalmist proclaimed in Psalm 34:4 that, *I sought the Lord, and he heard me, and delivered me from ALL my fears.* Go ahead. Tell God all about it. You don't have to pretend or hide the way you truly feel. He already knows. Try trusting Him to deliver you. You've tried everything else and everything else has failed. Try trusting God, knowing that *they that trust in the Lord shall be as mount Zion which cannot be removed, but abideth for ever* (Psalm 125:1). Nishan Panwar wrote, *If you live in fear of the future because of what happened in your past, you'll end up losing what you have in the present.*

If it will help, list your fears here. Then for each one of them that you list, write an appropriate scripture that demonstrates God's sovereignty over it. Remember the psalmist said after he sought God, God delivered him from ALL his fears.

Fear #1

Scripture:

_____
_____
_____
_____

Fear #2

_____
_____
_____
_____
_____
_____
_____
_____

Scripture:

_____
_____
_____
_____

Fear #3

_____
_____
_____
_____
_____
_____
_____
_____

Scripture:

_____
_____
_____
_____

Fear #4

_____
_____
_____
_____
_____
_____
_____
_____

Scripture

_____
_____
_____
_____

Chapter 13

A True Story

Let me share a true life story with you that I pray that will fuel your faith, strength, and belief in God's power to heal and restore. It highlights many of the major points I discussed in this book.

A young lady once shared with me how her failed relationships with men emotionally traumatized her. For the sake of keeping her identity anonymous, I will call her Cindy. The trauma Cindy experienced caused her to close her heart and become fearful of forming relationships. She said didn't trust men any more and felt that they were all alike, only wanting to use her sexually. As we discussed in chapter two, when trust is violated by an unfortunate event, it causes those bearing the emotional scars to become fearful of forming relationships with others.

Cindy told me how at the age of 16 she fell in love with her high school sweet heart. Not only was she very fond of him, but her family was as well. They were really in love and talked about getting married. Even though they were young at age, she felt that getting married was okay since both her parents and one of her siblings married young as well.

Eventually, they had relations outside of marriage. Little did Cindy know that he was a carrier of gonorrhea. She was devastated and crushed when she found out because she thought that her boyfriend loved her as much as she loved him. She felt betrayed and used by him. Even though he told her that he didn't know he had the disease, that did nothing to heal her broken heart or restore her trust in him.

Cindy even questioned God as to why He allowed this to happen to her. She was angry with herself and God. She felt that God did her unjustly. She knew of many girls in junior high school having sex and pregnant at the age 13; yet God didn't allow them to contact a venereal disease. In her own words, "She wanted God to grade her on the curve." She knew that having sex outside of marriage was wrong, but still she couldn't imagine something like this happening to her. After all, the young man said that he loved her, and she truly believed him.

Remember, another point I discussed in this book is how the pain of an ugly event causes the emotionally bruised to not only be angry with themselves, but also angry at God. They feel God has let them down by not protecting them.

Devastated by her first love's betrayal, Cindy eventually broke their relationship off. Her family wondered what happened because they really liked the young man. However, she felt too embarrassed to tell anyone about what had happened.

As I also discussed earlier in this book, many of the emotionally bruised are too embarrassed to tell others about what happened. They feel, as this young lady did, that others will look at them in another light and behave differently toward them.

After couple of years passed, Cindy met another guy and they dated for four years. She fell in love with him as well, but he only wanted her to satisfy the desires of his flesh. Eventually that relationship ended. With her heart crushed again, her self-esteem suffered greatly. She felt worthless, undeserving and vowed not to ever give her heart to another man. This caused her to "flip the script," if you will. Men to her became only a means by which she could satisfy her flesh. Satisfying the desires of her flesh became her way of dealing with her emotional pain (Remember, those who are emotionally wounded often turn to ungodly ways to deal with the hurt they experience). For about ten years, this is what she did. Cindy knew she was living outside of God's will, but the hurt she felt caused her to keep going.

But one day, Cindy became sick and tired of living the way she was living (Remember, a person who wants to receive inner healing has to be sick and tired of being bound and ready to reach out for help). She decided that she was going to give Jesus her broken heart one

Sunday. When the appeal was made for the altar call, Cindy ran down to the altar, with tears rolling down her face. She didn't care who saw her or that she had left her purse behind. She so badly wanted God to help her (Remember the chapter *How Bad Do You Want It?*)

This young lady asked God to come in to her heart and save her – from herself; from her condition. In her own words, "I felt trapped in a worldly lifestyle that I couldn't seem to break free from." Cindy felt powerless and asked God to help her to clean her life up because she knew she couldn't do it on her own. She said she felt like the woman did with the issue of blood, that if she could just touch the hem of Jesus' garment, that she would be made whole.

Those in need of healing must recognize that they need God's help in order to receive the true deliverance that they desire. On our own, we can do nothing (John 15:5).

Cindy vowed to God that if He delivered her this time, she wouldn't do the things that she had been doing that were contrary to His will. She went on to say that after she asked God to help her, she felt a change come over her. She felt her body being cleansed from all the old things of her past by God's wonder-working power. God not only cleansed her, but He forgave her, and healed her every where she was broken. God healed her of the intense inner pain she had carried for many years. Instead of relying on men to provide her with love, she began relying on Jesus, her "Solid Rock," to shower her with the love she needed. She said that with God's help healing and restoration was not just something she dreamt about, but it became a reality in her life.

Cindy went on to say that God also worked in her life, separating her from the old friends that she had. Instead of hanging out and going out with them, she began to attend church faithfully. Many times she would stay at home studying God's word. God also had her throw away any and all things that related to her past – movies, other DVDs, music, etc. He also changed her way of talking. Cindy said she felt like a new creature in Him. God truly ushered her into a new season in her life. She was so ecstatic as she shared the ending of her story to me! She didn't think she would ever smile again or love again! But with God in her equation, she was set free from the emotional chains holding her bound. Glory!

Therefore if any man be in Christ, he is a new creature: old things are passed away; behold, all things are become new. (2 Corinthians 5:17)

Chapter 14

Conclusion

Remember, healing from an emotional wound will take time. Of truth, God has the power to make us whole. He has the power to mend and restore us as if the unfortunate event never happened. He can do it instantly. But more often than not, it is a process. It will take time. Be patient with yourself and with God's work in you and for you. Know that God has heard your cry. The psalmist said in Psalm 40:1, *I waited patiently for the Lord and he inclined unto me, and heard my cry.*

Healing will also take persistence. Even after applying many of the tips that I mentioned in this book, you will find that it won't be as easy as 1, 2, 3 – that if you do this, then you will achieve that! Healing will be a process that will require you to be committed and dedicated to change. A process of successes and failures; hurts and pains; joy as you see glimpses of hope; and sorrow as it seems like some days you are not making progress. But, regardless, press on! Press beyond your urges to give up and days where you actually throw your hands up and say "Lord, I'm tired. What's the use?" Indeed, press on! There's a blessing, there's a healing, there's deliverance waiting for you on the other side of your press.

The Bible says, *But he that shall endure unto the end, the same shall be saved (Matthew 24:13)*. In the Greek, the word *saved* means to be healed, delivered, made whole, or rescued. Although this scripture refers to the end of time, it can also be generally applied in the case of emotional healing. If an individual endures and perseveres while God works His work, He shall be healed, delivered, and made whole. Glory!

Also remember, that admitting you have a problem is a BIG key to you getting the help you need. Can you imagine continuing in life, living as a "mummy," not being able to reach out, to move forward, or to reach your potential because your past is holding you captive? That's not an encouraging picture at all. You must first admit that you have a problem, and then others can help you. Then God can help.

Depending on the level of abuse that you have experienced, you may also need to seek professional help. Pray and ask God to lead and guide you if you feel you need professional help. There are even those who are trained and licensed in the Christian community to help walk you through the recovery process.

Remember also that talking to someone you really trust about your "secret" can be very helpful to you. If you keep it in, it will only affect you physically, mentally, emotionally, and spiritually. It will be like an "emotional cancer" that will spread to other areas of your life. There may be other well-meaning Christians who tell you to not talk about it. They believe that talking about it will only give room to the devil to cause more pain for you. But to you I say, "Talk about!" Tell God about it. He is our high priest which can be touched with the feelings of our infirmities yet without sin (Hebrews 4:15). Besides, He knows how it is to feel many of the sorrows that you and I have felt and are feeling. Isaiah 53:3 says, *He is despised and rejected of men: a man of sorrows, and acquainted with grief...* So tell God about it. Tell a confidante about it. Tell someone who is trained to help you about it. This will help relieve you of some of the stress, pain, and pressure that you may have been carrying.

Physical exercise can also help provide you relief from stress, anger and other pent up negative emotions that you have been dealing with. It will also help take your mind off of your situation. According to Dr. Darren Treasure,

> *Research over the past 10-15 years has shown that participation in moderate intensity exercise and physical activity is associated with improved emotion and mood states. These positive effects have been found for both aerobic (i.e. walking, cycling, and jogging and anaerobic activities (i.e. strength training). The biggest positive effect on emotions seems to be for those people who are currently feeling low with a single bout of exercise helping to alleviate negative emotion and feeling states.*

You may also want to get involved in one of your favorite hobbies as a way to take your mind off of your emotional distress. I recall many times when feeling overwhelmed. I would sit at the piano and just play whatever came to me. Sometimes it would be a song, and sometimes just chords in no certain order. I always would feel better after "tinkling the ivies." The anger, despair, frustration and discouragement would often subside.

Other times I would write a letter to God. It just always felt good to be able to write and tell Him EVERYTHING I was feeling – the good, the bad; the pretty, the ugly. Whatever I felt, I wrote it down, holding nothing back. I would feel so much better once I expressed myself to God in writing. This also made me feel really close to Him.

One of my favorite passages of scriptures I would read during times of great despair was Psalm 60:1-3,

> *Hear my cry, O God: attend unto my prayer, from the end of the earth will I cry unto thee, when my heart is overwhelmed: lead me to the rock that is higher than I.*

Whatever you do to help you deal with the distress caused by your emotional wound, just don't give up! God is standing by and He does want to help you.

Also, remember you can't change your past. However, you can learn from your past and use it to help someone. Consider becoming an advocate for others dealing with an issue similar to yours. Others need to hear your testimony. They need to see that they are not alone in their struggles. Your testimony just may save someone's life! God did not allow you to go through what you went through for naught. He always has a master plan. God has double in store for you for your trouble (Isaiah 61:3)!

As I close, I would like you to leave you with the lyrics of one of my favorite songs. I found strength and comfort listening to it each time my soul was in the valley of despair. It is a song entitled *Healing* by Richard Smallwood. It says,

Don't be discouraged
Joy comes in the morning
Know that God is nigh
Stand still and look up
God is going to show up
He is standing by

There's healing for your sorrow
Healing for your pain
Healing for your spirit
There's shelter from the rain

Lord send the healing
For this we know
There is a balm in Gilead
For there's a balm in Gilead
There is a balm in Gilead
To heal the soul
Healing for the soul

Additional Scriptures of Comfort

All throughout this book, I purposely quoted many scriptures for it is by the life-changing power of God's word that your life can be changed for the better. Here I have listed additional scriptures that can serve as a source of encouragement, strength and hope for you as you walk toward your freedom. The word of God is life and it gives life – life to the hopeless; life to the bound; life to the oppressed.

So read, believe, and hold on to God's unchanging word. It may not "appear" to be changing you or your condition, but with God we walk by faith and not by sight (2 Corinthians 5:7). As you apply the word in faith, it will work on your behalf.

Psalm 120:1
In my distress I cried unto the Lord, and he heard me.

Hebrew 4:15-16
For we have not a high priest which cannot be touched with the feeling of our infirmities; but was in all points tempted like as we are, yet without sin.

Let us therefore come boldly unto the throne of grace, that we may obtain mercy, and find grace to help in time of need.

Psalm 18:17

He delivered me from my strong enemy and from them which hate me: for they were too strong for me.

Psalm 24:7-8
Lift up your heads, O ye gates; and be ye lift up, ye everlasting doors; and the King of glory shall come in. Who is this King of glory? The Lord strong and mighty, the Lord mighty in battle.

Psalm 121:1-3
I will lift up mine eyes unto the hills, from whence cometh my help. My help cometh from the Lord, which made heaven and earth. He will not suffer thy foot to be moved: he that keepeth thee will not slumber.

Psalm 121:7
The Lord shall preserve therefrom all evil: he shall preserve thy soul.

1 Corinthians 15:57
But thanks be to God, which giveth us the victory through our Lord Jesus Christ.

2 Corinthians 3:14
Now thanks be unto God, which always causeth us to triumph in Christ, and maketh manifest the savour of his knowledge by us in every place.

Mark 13:31
Heaven and earth shall pass away: but my words shall not pass away.

Hebrews 4:12

For the word of God is quick, and powerful, and sharper than any two-edged sword, piercing even to the dividing asunder of soul and spirit, and of the joints and marrow, and is a discerner of the thoughts and intents of the heart.

Isaiah 55:11
So shall my word be that goeth forth out of my mouth: it shall not return unto me void, but it shall accomplish that which I please, and it shall prosper in the thing whereto I sent it.

Bibliography

Emotional detachment. Wikipedia. Retrieved May 9, 2014, from http://en.wikipedia.org/wiki/Emotional_detachment.

Meyers, Joyce. *Beauty for Ashes — Receiving Emotional Healing.* Harrison House, Tulsa, Oklahoma, 1994.

Moore, Thomas. www.goodreads.com. 6 June 2014

Panwar, Nishan. www.searchquotes.com. 6 June 2014.

Spryszak, Monique. What is Ostracism? http://www.ostracism-awareness.com. 30 April 2014.

Treasure, Darren. "Will Exercise Help My Emotions?" *Sharecare*.com. Nike SPARQ Training Network, Sportsmedicine, Web. 7 June 2014.

Winch, Guy. "5 Tips for Recovering from Emotional Pain." *CNN.com.* Cable News Network, 2 Aug. 2013. 6 June 2014.

Winch, Guy. "5 tips for healing emotional pain. Mercola.com. 15 Aug. 2013. 9 May 2014.

Other books by Dr. Demetria Springfield Banks:

Books:
25 Workplace Survival Tips for the Believer
Prayer Pearls: Priceless Inspiration
Every Single One of You: Living Above Single Life Frustrations
20 Prayers for the Workplace
I Am Somebody That's Who I Am
Between the Watch, the Wait and God's Work

To contact the author, please write:
DSB Life Solutions, LLC
P.O. Box 1877
Memphis, TN 38101
Internet address: www.demetriasbanks.com
Email: office@demetriasbanks.com